Sports Legends

BY SUSAN BROCKER

TABLE OF CONTENTS

INTRODUCTION 2
CHAPTER 1 Babe Didrikson Zaharias: Amazing Athlete 4
CHAPTER 2 Pelé: Soccer King 10
CHAPTER 3 Lance Armstrong: Cycling Superstar 16
FOR THE RECORD 22
GLOSSARY 23
INDEX 24

Introduction

There are many famous sports figures. Some are athletes who have broken world records and won gold medals. But only a few can be called sports legends. Sports legends are remembered for a long time. They leave something behind long after their wins have been forgotten.

Soccer king Pelé (1940–)

Amazing athlete Babe Didrikson Zaharias (1911–1956)

The three people you will read about in this book—Babe Didrikson Zaharias (DEE-drik-sun Zuh-HAR-ee-uhz), Pelé (Peh-LAY), and Lance Armstrong—are all sports legends. Each is an amazing athlete. More important, each has shown great courage and spirit. They make us want to try harder—not just in sports, but in everything we do.

Cycling superstar Lance Armstrong (1971–)

Babe Didrikson Zaharias

AMAZING ATHLETE

The crowd cheered as Babe cleared the hurdles to break her fourth world record of the day. On her own, she had scored enough points to win the track **meet** for her entire team. She had also qualified for the Olympic Games.

Babe Didrikson Zaharias was surely the greatest all-around athlete of her time. She was an Olympic track-and-field medal winner and a **champion** golfer. She also competed in basketball, baseball, bowling, tennis, diving, and swimming.

Babe was born in Port Arthur, Texas, in 1911. One of seven children, she loved playing sports with her brothers. She usually won the games. She could outrun and outthrow all the boys. But Babe had to work hard to be the best. She spent hours lifting weights made from broomsticks and old irons.

Babe's real name was Mildred. She was given the nickname "Babe" after baseball legend Babe Ruth. Like him, Babe hit many home runs.

Golf began as a sport for only those who had both the time and the money to devote to it.

Today, children and adults alike are able to enjoy golf.

javelin

basketball

Babe was an all-around athlete. She played in many sports.

shot put

It's a FACT!

The first modern Olympic Games were held in Athens, Greece, in 1896. Women were not allowed to compete. The rule was changed for the next Olympics in 1900 in Paris. Women competed in croquet, golf, and tennis. They were not allowed to compete in track and field until 1928. Today, most Olympic sports have both men's and women's events.

Babe played every sport during her high school years. The basketball team never lost a game while Babe was on the team. When Babe graduated, she went to work for a company in Dallas, Texas, so that she could play on its basketball team. She was named an all-American player three years in a row.

Babe began to compete in track and field during her late teens. She was not popular with her teammates or the public at first. They thought she was too confident for a female athlete.

But when Babe played in the 1932 Olympic Games in Los Angeles, California, people changed their minds. Babe qualified in five events! According to Olympic rules, however, she was allowed to compete in only three events. Babe won gold medals in the javelin throw and the 80-meter hurdles. She won a silver medal in the high jump.

Babe, on the right, was on her way to capturing the gold medal in the 80-meter hurdles at the 1932 Olympic Games.

✔ Point

THINK IT OVER

Why do you think the Olympic rules limited the number of events women athletes could compete in?

After the Olympic Games, Babe started playing golf. It was one of the few sports in which women could earn a living. She practiced every day, hitting balls until her hands hurt. She was as good at golf as she was at her other sports.

Between 1946 and 1947, Babe won 17 **amateur** (AM-ah-choor) tournaments in a row. She did not receive any money for her participation. Soon after, she turned **professional** and helped set up the women's **circuit** (SUR-kit). She was its star and leading money winner.

In 1953, Babe had surgery for cancer. Her doctors told her she would never play championship golf again. But less than a year later, Babe won the U.S. Women's Open for the third time by a record 12 strokes. Her courage and spirit made her a hero to many people.

Grantland Rice, a well-known American sportswriter, was very important in Babe's life. He encouraged her to play golf and gave her a lot of support during her career.

Babe died from cancer in 1956. She left behind a record of sports achievements unmatched even today. She also left behind an amazing story of courage and perseverance.

THEN & NOW

Golf has been played for hundreds of years. While the rules of the game have not changed since 1744, the equipment has! Early golfers played with a leather ball stuffed with feathers. The clubs were made of wood. Today, the balls are much harder and golfers play with clubs made of lighter materials.

Babe's powerful swing changed the way women played golf and made the game more popular.

Pelé

SOCCER KING

It was the semifinal game of the 1958 soccer World Cup. As the teenager from Brazil scored a **hat trick,** or three goals in one game, the fans went wild. The talented 17-year-old would go on to score two goals in the final game. He would lead his team to victory and become the youngest World Cup winner.

From that day on, Pelé was known as the "king of soccer." During his career, he scored more than 1,200 goals! He made soccer a popular sport in the United States. On and off the field, Pelé is a hero to millions of people.

Pelé was born in 1940 in a small village in Brazil. His family was poor. He learned to play soccer with a ball made of old socks. All Pelé wanted to do was play soccer. Every day he practiced barefoot on the streets with the other boys.

Pelé's real name is Edson Arantes do Nascimento (ED-sohn Ah-RAN-tez doh Nah-see-MEN-to). He got the name Pelé while playing soccer with his friends. Although its meaning is not certain, it's become the most famous name in sports history.

Today, young and old alike can enjoy soccer.

Originally, soccer required only comfortable clothing, a ball, and a grassy field.

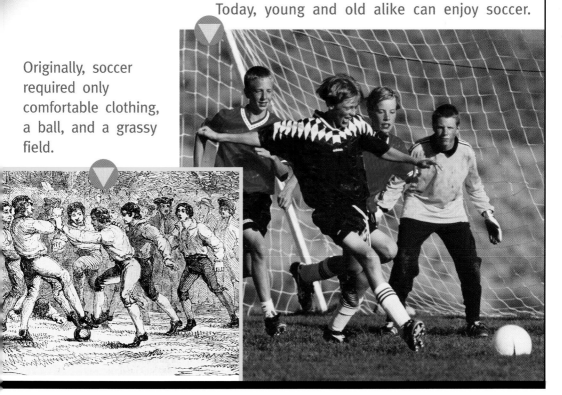

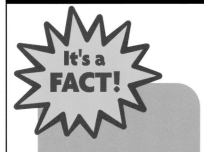

It's a FACT!

Soccer is the world's most popular sport. Every four years, teams from around the globe play for the World Cup. In 1970, Pelé played in the World Cup final against Italy. About 900 million people watched the game on television.

When Pelé was 15, he signed to play professional soccer with the Santos Club of Brazil. He led the team to a record number of wins. He played **forward** in his number-10 shirt, which soon became famous.

A year later, Pelé put on the yellow shirt of Team Brazil. With Pelé on the team, Brazil won its first World Cup in 1958. They won it again in 1962 and in 1970. Pelé is the only soccer player to have played on three winning World Cup teams.

This is the 1958 World Cup-winning Brazilian Team. Can you find Pelé? If you need help, he's in the front row, the third from the left.

Pelé was a great player. He had speed, grace, and **agility** (uh-JILL-uh-tee). He could control the ball while running. He could shoot it with either foot or with his head. He could even hook the ball back over his head to score a goal. But Pelé not only scored amazing goals, he also made chances for others to score.

Pelé was "discovered" when he was 11 years old by Brazilian soccer coach Valdemar de Brito. He taught Pelé many skills, including the bicycle kick. De Brito also helped Pelé get on the Santos team.

THEN & NOW

In 1975, the president of the professional soccer team called the New York Cosmos talked Pelé into coming to the U.S. to play for the team. Pelé became a big star. He drew record crowds to his games. Children all over the country wanted to play soccer. In 1977, Pelé led the Cosmos to the **league** championship.

That same year, thousands watched Pelé play his last match. The game was between the Cosmos and his old team, the Santos. He played the first half for the Cosmos and the second half for the Santos.

Pelé played his first game for the New York Cosmos against the Dallas Tornadoes.

At the opening of a sports school in Brazil in 1997, Pelé shows President Clinton how to kick a soccer ball.

Pelé has always believed that sports bring people together. Since he retired in 1977, he has worked to set up soccer **clinics** for children in poor areas of Brazil. There, children learn to play the game and play as a team. Pelé also works for many children's causes. The "king of soccer" has never forgotten what it was like growing up poor, playing with a ball made of old socks.

Lance Armstrong

CYCLING SUPERSTAR

Fans lined the streets of Paris to cheer on the brave cyclist as he crossed the finish line. Lance Armstrong had won the 1999 Tour de France, the hardest of all bicycle races. He had done it in record time. He had gone more than 2,200 miles in three weeks. His win came at the end of a long battle against cancer. His comeback is one of the bravest stories in the history of sports.

Lance Armstrong was born in Plano, Texas, in 1971. As a boy, he was very strong and had lots of spirit. He competed in triathlons (try-ATH-lonz), events that combine swimming, cycling, and running. When he was 13, he won the Iron Kids Triathlon. At 16, he turned professional.

The first bicycle was invented in 1817. It was made of wood and had no pedals. The rider pushed it with his feet. When the all-metal bicycles with pedals were introduced in the 1860s, they were very costly. Few people could afford to buy them.

Today, many people enjoy bike riding.

THEN & NOW

The first bicycle race was held in France in 1868. In those days, bicycles had a big front wheel and a small back wheel. The seat was over the front wheel. The bikes were difficult to ride. The first modern bike, with a chain link and wheels of the same size, was made in 1879. Since then, changes in design have made bikes faster. Today, bikes are made of very lightweight materials. There are different kinds of bikes for different kinds of racing. They include road, track, and mountain bikes.

While in high school, Lance decided that he wanted to race bikes. By his last year, he had qualified to train with the U.S. Olympic cycling team. After graduating, he spent almost all his time racing. By 1991 he was the U.S. National Amateur Champion. A year later he biked at the Olympic Games in Barcelona, Spain.

Lance turned professional after the Olympic Games. Although he came in last in his first race, he did not quit. Instead, he trained harder. In 1993 he won 10 big **titles**. During the World Road Race Championship in Norway, Lance crashed twice on roads made slippery by rain. But he still won the race. He won the Tour Du Pont, the best-known cycle race in the United States, in 1995 and 1996. People were calling him the "golden boy" of American cycling.

Lance leads the pack as he nears the finish line.

In 1996, Lance learned that he had cancer. He was frightened, but he was set on fighting the disease. With the support of his family and friends, he started treatment. He had made up his mind that he would race again. Lance set his sights on the greatest road race of all—the Tour de France. He trained daily in the mountains. He worked hard to get stronger.

Lance leads his fellow bikers after winning the Tour de France.

In July 1999, Lance Armstrong amazed the world by winning the race. He was more than seven minutes ahead of everyone else.

Against all odds, Lance won the Tour de France again in 2000, 2001, 2002, and 2003. He is the first American to have won the race five times in a row. He is a symbol of hope for people who face cancer. He is a true sports legend.

Lance's hero is his mother, Linda. As a single parent, she raised Lance, worked hard to support him, and cheered him on at every sports event. She taught Lance to never give up.

**Point**

THINK IT OVER

Make a list of your favorite sports figures. Could any people on your list be called a sports legend today? Will any be called a sports legend in the future? Explain your answer.

For the Record

BABE DIDRIKSON ZAHARIAS

- 1932 Olympic Games gold-medal winner in 80-meter hurdles with world-record time of 11.7 seconds
- 1932 Olympic Games gold-medal winner in javelin with throw of 143 feet, 4 inches
- 1932 Olympic Games silver-medal winner in high jump with jump of 5 feet, 5 inches
- Won U.S. Women's Open in 1948, 1950, and 1954

PELÉ

- Holds every major scoring record for soccer in Brazil
- Scored 1,281 goals in 1,363 professional games
- Only player to have played on three World Cup championship teams: 1958, 1962, and 1970
- Youngest scorer in a World Cup final

LANCE ARMSTRONG

- World Professional Road Race champion in 1993
- Tour Du Pont champion in 1995 and 1996
- Tour de France champion in 1999, with record-breaking average speed of 25.026 miles per hour
- Tour de France champion in 2000, 2001, 2002, and 2003

Glossary

agility	(uh-JILL-uh-tee) the ability to move quickly and easily (page 13)
amateur	(AM-ah-choor) an event that is not professional (page 8)
champion	(CHAM-pee-un) a person who wins first place or is judged to be the best (page 4)
circuit	(SUR-kit) a course or series of events (page 8)
clinic	(KLIN-ik) a place where people can go to get instruction or advice for a certain sport (page 15)
forward	(FOR-wurd) an offensive position in soccer (page 12)
hat trick	(HAT trik) scoring three goals in one game (page 10)
league	(leeg) a group of teams in a particular sport that compete mostly against one another (page 14)
meet	(meet) a competition for a particular sport (page 4)
professional	(pro-FESH-uh-null) a person who is paid for his/her great skill at something (page 8)
title	(TYT-ull) a word or name showing the rank of a person (page 19)

Index

agility, 13
amateur, 8
Armstrong, Lance, 16–22
champion, 4, 22
circuit, 8
clinic, 15
cycling, 16–19
forward, 12
golf, 5, 8–9
hat trick, 10
league, 14
meet, 4
New York Cosmos, 14
Olympic Games, 4, 6–8, 18–19, 22

Pelé, 10–15, 22
professional, 8, 12, 19, 22
Rice, Grantland, 8
Santos Club, 12
soccer, 10–15, 22
title, 19
Tour de France, 16, 20–22
Tour Du Pont, 19
track and field, 4, 6–7
triathlon, 17
U.S. Women's Open, 8, 22
World Cup, 10, 12, 22
Zaharias, Babe Didrikson, 4–9, 22